ON

Memorizing and Playing from Memory

and on the Laws of Practice generally

By TOBIAS MATTHAY

Music Department
OXFORD UNIVERSITY PRESS
44 Conduit Street, London W.1

First Published 1926
Ninth Impression 1972

FOREWORD

In my various publications and lectures I have already alluded to the processes of Memorizing and Playing from Memory; but I feel that all this matter should now be brought more into focus: hence the publication of the present booklet. It forms the fifth of my series of "Six Lectures to Teachers on the Psychology of Teaching", first written during the summer of 1919, and as since given at my School for the "Teacher's Training Course" classes and elsewhere.

Needless to point out that these laws of memorizing and making use of memory do not apply solely to playing "without the book". On the contrary, these same laws apply during every moment of every practice-hour; and they apply not only while "learning the notes" of a piece, but they apply also every moment subsequently, during the preparation of a performance, and again during actual performance—whether with the book or without. Indeed, the processes described apply to the learning and retention of anything and everything.

TOBIAS MATTHAY.

Haslemere,

January 1926.

CONTENTS

AN INTRODUCTION TO PSYCHOLOGY FOR TEACHERS

LECTURE No. V

ON

MEMORIZING AND PLAYING FROM MEMORY

ON ASSOCIATION AND OBSERVATION, ETC. AND ON THE LAWS OF PRACTICE, GENERALLY

By TOBIAS MATTHAY

We have in previous lectures considered the element of Attention and Interest, and the related one of Analysis, and have touched upon that of Association and Observation. Clearly, the question of memorizing, and playing from memory, is closely related to all these. In speaking of Memorizing, some of you may say: "But this is quite a subsidiary issue; we are not going to insist on all our pupils playing from memory, from the very beginning!" You cannot make a greater mistake. The question of memorizing is a *first* and *last* one in all teaching, and in all learning and practising.

Unless you understand the nature of memorizing, you cannot, for instance, learn merely the notes of a piece in the quickest and most efficacious way! In fact, the acquisition of any knowledge always implies "memorizing"—even when you do not propose to speak or play eventually without the book.

Nothing learnt without memorizing

We will first take the subject of Memorizing, or committing to memory, and afterwards that of Memory-use, or playing from memory.

Of course you all know that, with regard to Memory, people may be placed into three different categories:

1 The person who memorizes *instantaneously*, and *never* forgets.
2 The one who memorizes *slowly* but surely, but never forgets; and lastly—
3 The unfortunate, who memorizes with much painful labour—but forgets almost immediately!

Great artists there have been under both of the first two categories. No one suffering under the third should ever attempt a public career as performer—it would only make for life-long misery! Anyway, he should give up all idea of playing from memory! Whichever category, however, you may belong to, your work will be all the better for a little consideration of the rationale of memorizing or learning.

To begin with, let us disabuse ourselves of the popular but fallacious notion, that recalling something implies that something re-begins to exist in our mind which had ceased to exist. In short, realize that if we have a memory of something, it simply implies a *continuity* of something. In other words, an impression once made does not die off, and then re-live. The impression simply remains alive, although, maybe, the mind becomes sleepy with regard to its presence. As A. A. Lindsay has well put it, "to understand memory we should try to understand forgetting".* We find, after receiving an impression, that it fades rapidly at first; but after that, the further fading takes gradually longer and longer in its steps of enfeeblement. In fact, one cannot say that an impression once made ever completely fades from the tablets of the mind. But more on this point later on.†

ALEXANDER BAIN puts this very clearly in his "Mind and Body—the Theories of their Relation", a fine book published in the "International Science Series" by Paul Trench & Co. Some may perhaps consider this to be rather out of date now, but it is not so in my opinion. Bain says, page 89, on "Retention, Acquisition, or Memory": . . . "being the power of continuing in the mind "impressions that *are no longer* stimulated by the original agent, "and of recalling them (at after times) by purely mental forces. I "shall remark first on the cerebral seat of those renewed impres-"sions. It must be considered as almost beyond a doubt that *the "renewed feeling occupies the very same parts (of the physical "brain) and in the same manner as the original feeling*, and no "other parts, nor in any other manner that can be assigned. . . . If "we suppose the sound of a bell striking the ear, which then ceases "sounding, there is a certain continuing impression of a feebler "kind, the idea or memory of the note of the bell; and it would "take some very good reason to deter us from the obvious "inference *that the continuing* impression *is the persisting* (although

*A. A. Lindsay, "Pearls of Psychology" page 79. Lindsay Publishing Co , San Francisco, U.S.A.

†*See* Additional Note, "On Memory Scratches," page 17.

"reduced) nerve-currents aroused by the original shock. . . "The mental recollection of language is a suppressed articulation, "ready to burst into speech. When the thought of an action "excites us very much, we can hardly avoid the actual repetition "[of the action] so completely are all the nervous circuits re-"possessed with the original currents of force. . . . Moreover, it "has been determined by experiment (for instance) that the "persistent imagination of a bright colour fatigues the nerves of "sight". You should read more of Bain yourselves.

Routine.

I must explain that I do not here propose to discuss which *routine* is the best to be followed in committing a thing to memory—whether it is best to present to the mind at once the whole thing to be memorized, or only parts at a time, or for how long at a time one should thus persist in making the presentation—in trying to make the impression. Personally, I believe the routine must differ with each individual, and with the nature of the thing to be memorized. But there is no doubt that persisting *too long at a time* (with one particular presentation) will fatigue rather than help—just as in the muscular analogy. One cannot strengthen one's muscles, nor can one strengthen one's mental-muscular habits, except by frequent and short exercises; therefore one cannot fix a passage in the memory by over-long presentation at one time. Moreover, no presentation can be useful to the mind unless it is analysed. Let me quote you a few lines from Robert Louis Stevenson which bear upon this point:

"Mark the note that rises,
Mark the notes that fall,
Mark the time when broken,
And the swing of it all;

So when night is come
And you are gone to bed,
All the songs you love to sing
Will echo in your head."

You see the poet says, "*mark*" the things you wish to remember —analyse them, note them!

For information as to the "Routine" of learning, I would urge you all to refer to a work recently published: "The Psychology of Education," by David Kennedy-Fraser (Methuen).

What I wish to do here is to try to make clear to you the *nature* of the process itself of memorizing; and also the reverse process, that of playing from memory. Here realize, in the first place, that the *act* of playing from memory is purely an *automatic* action of the brain. Recalling something means that our brain has formed an automatic sequential action in that respect.

The distinction between Memory fixing and using.

But the act of *committing to memory* is precisely the reverse process—it is a compelled action. In short, the action of the memory is automatic, whereas the act of committing to memory is more or less consciously a wilful one. Moreover, the Act of Playing, itself, *must always be willed!*—otherwise you cannot make any musical impression.

Memorizing, from its *physical* aspect, is obviously a change of state in the grey matter of the brain. It may be pictured as the forming of physical fibrous connexions or channels between one brain corpuscle and another—so that when one corpuscle is excited this excitation is transmitted to any other corpuscles that may have been thus connected-up by such physical fibrous channels.

The process of memorizing may thus be said to consist, physically, in the making and strengthening of such physical connexions or channels, or *ways* in the mind. Remember that!

The moral to be realized is, that facts, so long as they are *isolated*, mean nothing. Therefore, to memorize anything, the only possible process is to bring the something you wish to memorize into some form of connexion, progression, or sequence of thought. Here I will quote from my own "Musical Interpretation"* "On Memorizing" (page 41, etc.), as follows: "that is, you must chain the something you want to fix in your mind to something already stored there; you must make use of something you already know, so that it shall suggest (as a mental progression) the something fresh which you want to fix in your memory. You see, we here again come back to the Element of Progression!

Memory implies Association.

"In short, to the knowledge you already possess, you must build-on further progressions of 'onwardness' mentally—new Sequential Actions mentally.

"In the case of Musical-memory, each note, each chord you play, must be made to suggest the next note or next chord, etc.

*"Musical Interpretation, its Laws and Principles." (Joseph Williams.)

And unless you have made a perfect chain of such *suggestion-connexions*, you do not remember and cannot remember any piece—or anything else. In short, remembrance of a piece means that the suggestion-channels are all in good working order". The point to realize is, that in memorizing it is useless to try to "memorize" the thing we wish to note, as such—as an isolated thing, as an entity in itself. That is waste of time. We can only successfully note a thing by our fixing up for it an association, a connexion in thought with other things—that is, an association with other things, other thoughts, and experiences already present in our brain. The secret of Mneumonics is that we must note, must realize the *whence* for each musical thing; we must make a relation for it in our minds, so that when its relative, the preceding note, etc., is sounded, this relative will then automatically call up a consecution to the next note, etc., and thus we find it to be fixed in our mind—in fact, *memorized.*

In performance, allow memory to act

*Vice versa,** successfully to make use of the memory-connexions thus stored in our mind, we must (during performance) allow the thing present (the thing realized at the moment) to suggest the thing which is to follow on. That is, we must *allow* the memory of each coming portion of the text to be automatically revived by the rhythmic swing of the portion of the passage we *are* playing at the moment—its melodic and harmonic progression, its mood, and each note.

In short, each portion of the passage we *are* playing must successfully and successively revive each next progression of melody, harmony, mood, and each actual note. *That is, we must allow Association to assert its force.* Let me demonstrate this point at the Pianoforte, taking a Chopin Nocturne (the early one in G minor), showing you the process pursued in memorizing passages by the analysis of their melodic, harmonic and rhythmic constituents of musical progression. In learning the melodic progressions, for instance, it is not a row of detached notes—a mere succession of notes which you should try to fix in your mind, but instead, the true melodic connexions of these notes; in a word, you should note *the intervals substended between the notes.* A melody is not a succession of notes, but is "a succession of INTERVALS, rhythmically shaped", as I have said elsewhere. Learn the intervals—the movements in pitch—and you learn the tunes, musically. To learn to play them you must, in addition, learn these

*From "Musical Interpretation", page 42.

intervals of tunes as intervals of space on the Pianoforte keyboard, as you will see presently.

(This was illustrated at the pianoforte.)

TO RESTATE ALL THIS: When playing, you must *allow* your consciousness, or memory-stream, to flow in the channels, or courses, ways, or notes which you have previously made for it. *Vice versa*, the only way to prompt these memory-connexions into action is by keeping your mind vividly present *on the actual thing you are doing at the moment.*

You cannot help your memory during performance by trying to recall the thing ahead; on the contrary, this will inevitably disconnect and destroy the sequential action of your mind—that sequential action which we term "Memory", and you will break down.

On trying to recall the "next note".

The moment you begin to doubt your memory's capacity thus to "follow on", that moment you will hinder, if not completely stop, its continuity of action. Thus, if you commit the fatal blunder of *trying to recall the next note*, this will at once paralyse the natural and safe action of the previously-made sequential memory-ways or channels. You will thus stop the flow of your mind—the movement of your mind—and your mind will seem to be a blank as to what comes next. Here it is not a case of your memory being incomplete or unreliable, but simply that you are *preventing* its natural action.

Either the mental associations of "onwardness of Movement" are there, or they are not! If they are complete, they will act with certainty, provided you *allow* them thus to act; whereas, if they are not properly fixed in your mind, then no attempt to recall the *next* note will help you one jot!*

Remember, in this connexion, DARWIN's experiment on his lecture-class. He had postulated that if you wilfully *try to provoke* what has become an *automatic* action in response to a

*Illustrating this point—the course of the memory being stopped by one's "trying to remember the next thing": At one of our private concert meetings one of the performers broke down after playing about 16 bars. She then started again and broke down after playing only eight bars. Again she tried, and again stopped herself, after four bars now. Finally, after being urged to play again, she was only able to play the first four notes! I then pulled her together by speaking to her from the audience, saying: "Do not *try* to remember, but just think the music, and let the music take you along". She then started once more and quite successfully played the same little Purcell piece to the end, without hesitation. She had been *preventing* the natural memory-action of her mind, and *stopping* it by asking herself: "What is the next note?".

particular stimulus, then that automatic action will fail. He then told his class they could not sneeze *if they tried* to do so—and passed his snuff-box round. Not one of the class, however, could manage a sneeze, since they all tried their hardest to produce this action wilfully in answer to his challenge. Yet without that wilful interference with an automatic-sequential action, they would all probably have had paroxysms of automatically respondent sneezing!

To sum this up: If your musical mental connexions (or chains) have been properly linked up, you can only stimulate them into action by bringing your attention vividly upon the point you *are* engaged upon at each moment during the performance of the piece—so that each item may suggest the following one. Whereas, you will inevitably destroy or paralyse this natural, sequential action if you try to wrench your mind on to something ahead, something not yet actually due in performance.

On the other hand, if these progression-suggestions are not firmly fixed in your mind, then you must take steps to strengthen them, on the lines here indicated.

Much bad playing, such as the stumbling and stuttering so often found with students, usually arises directly from non-comprehension of this fact that all memorizing (whatever its nature) can only be achieved by impressing upon our mind the requisite and correct *progressions*, sequences, continuities or chains of succession of the music, in all its details.

Good and bad fault-correction.

For this reason, again, the teacher must never allow a pupil to try to "correct" a fault (whether slip of finger, wrong note, wrong time, tone, or duration) by his playing the right effect *after* the wrong one. Note this point!

(An example was here given at the pianoforte.)

It must be made plain that so far from being a correction, such proceeding forms what may indeed be called Un-practice, or Dis-practice, for it is a disruption of the correct musical successions. By playing the right note in succession after the wrong one we obviously tend to impress a totally *wrong sequence* upon our minds; and we shall therefore risk repeating the blunder with its supposed correction the very next time we play that passage; and if we repeat it we shall be a good way towards *ensuring* a stumble or stutter at that place.

The only true correction of a fault is to substitute the *correct succession* of sounds for the wrong succession; the only way is to go back, and *move across* the damaged place while carefully omitting the hiatus. Thus only can a new and correct mental succession be set up. I will read you presently one of my "Teaching Problems" on this point. Refer again to Additional Note, "On Memory Scratches", page 18.

The various forms of Memory available.

Here it is well to realize that musical memory is a complex phenomenon. We must realize that there are quite a number of distinct forms of memory available in playing. These can only be rendered available by the application of close *analysis* purposely or instinctively given in each direction. These components of memory are on the one side purely musical, but on the other side they are technical, instrumental, and muscular—or gynmastical. Thus, we must analyse (and thus memorize) the MUSICAL progressions of the piece; we must analyse its rhythmical, its melodic, and its harmonic progressions, and above all things analyse the inflexions of its moods, or poetic curves. But besides such, strictly speaking, musical memorizing of the piece, we must also impress our EYE-MEMORY with the picture of the written page, and the Eye-memory also with the *lie* of the music *on the keyboard*—that is, with the look of the keyboard progressions.

Moreover, added to all this, we must also apply our MUSCULAR-MEMORY, that is, we must fix in our mind the physical sensations of the note-successions upon the keyboard, and the sensations of the technical processes occasioning their execution.

Eight forms of Memory used in playing

To sum this up: We find there are *three* main forms of Memory used in playing:

1 THE MUSICAL.
2 THE VISUAL.
3 THE MUSCULAR.

But as each of these can appeal to us in several quite distinct ways, we may say there are at least *eight* diverse memory-channels which may help us. Thus:

1. *The Musical Memory:* this divides into Melodic, Harmonic, Rhythmical, and Moodal memory, and this last includes the required inflexual memory of the Tone, Time, and Duration inflexions. All these four are forms of *Musical* Memory.

2. *The Visual Memory:* includes (*a*) Eye-memory of the page, and (*b*) Eye-memory of the keyboard progressions and combinations.

3. *The Muscular Memory:* comprises (*a*) The sense of *Place* and movement from note to note—the spaces traversed—*on the keyboard*, and (*b*) the sense of Key-motion (key-resistance)—the

going down, and also the coming up, of the key—the duration-sensation.

Thus we have *four* forms of memory under "Musical", and *two* under "Visual", and *two* under "Muscular".

You should note these facts, they will prove helpful in your own practice, and useful also when you try to help others to learn. Remember, a mental connecting-up or "chaining-on" can be accomplished in all these eight distinct ways, and, moreover, it always implies *analysis* in each case.

The Muscular Memory and its dangers.

Just now I spoke of *Muscular Memory*. Now it is just here where trouble often begins. On the one hand, it is impossible to give our mind to the musical interpretation of a *quick* movement unless we "know the notes" of it so well that we need no longer question what they are. To succeed in this, however (in a quick movement), we must have repeated its note-successions often enough to impress them thoroughly upon our automatic-centres, so that our "fingers" may *seem* to find the road automatically.

The imminent danger, however, always facing us here, is that in trying to acquire this necessary automatic part of the performance-memory, we may in the meantime totally destroy all our musical control over the piece, and allow ourselves actually to *play* automatically! It is this very necessity of automatic note-memory which so often leads players astray into the acquisition of purely automatic and mechanical methods of practice and playing. Remember: Memory must be automatic in its action, but Performance must *never* be so.

The only remedy and preventive, here, is constantly to insist on real *musical attention* through the Time-impulse. Practice, *away from the keyboard*, should also be insisted upon. When our fingers are upon the keyboard it is only too easy to forget to direct them musically, hence the great value of silent practice, without playing a note, but with every note-inflexion and the actual playing processes vividly imagined. During such silent practice it is impossible to allow the attention to slacken even for a moment.

And when actual keyboard-practice is imperative, during the process of acquiring or reviving the necessary automaticity in respect to the keyboard-successions of the notes, even in this case we must never allow our automatic (or gymnastic) faculty to gain the upper hand; we must never allow it to fulfil its sway without our constantly directing and controlling it *musically*, by our *mind-*

centres—our will-power, our musical imagination and judgement —our Time judgement, and our Tone judgement.

On Harmonic Analysis.

Moreover, the musical process in making such memory-channels, memory-ways, or memory-routes depends largely on harmonic analysis, and particularly upon our understanding clearly which are the fundamental harmony notes and which are ornamentations. To make this clear let me give you an example of how to analyse a passage. We will take these four bars from Chopin's B minor Scherzo. Here we have simply the harmony of G minor followed by the dominant and tonic harmonies of D major, but disguised by ornamental notes at (⊕):

EXP. 1. CHOPIN, SCHERZO

Unless these ornamentations are recognized as such, the true harmonic scheme remains obscure, and therefore difficult to memorize, and also difficult to make clear to the listener, since the listener must be made to feel these passing notes moving to their resolutions. In the opening bars of the same Scherzo we have similar problems to realize. The ornamental notes and their resolutions are indicated in the following example:

EXP. 2. CHOPIN, SCHERZO.

The *coda* from the first movement of the Sonata, Op. 110, Beethoven, furnishes a slightly more complex example of passing notes with deferred resolutions and overlapping. Unless all this is recognized, neither can the passage be made clear nor can it be easily learnt. Notice how the composer here not only uses both alternative passing notes, but hovers between them before resolving them. Example:

EXP. 3. BEETHOVEN, Op. 110.

To quote again from "Musical Interpretation" (page 44):

To revive rhythmical vision.

"Control over a passage means rhythmical control, and to gain this, and keep this, we must constantly re-analyse the *rhythmical* Constituents or rhythmical *Landmarks* of every agility-piece, however old an acquaintance it may be. The moment we thus insist on compelling the automatic centres to *fit their work* to our rhythmical vision, that moment the piece no longer seems to 'run away', but instead can be perfectly guided by our musical conscience. Hence, in performance, we must also always insist on realizing the *time-place* for each note or group of notes; and doing so, our gymnastic faculty then becomes our obedient servant, not our master". To prevent such "slithering" of passages (or sliding along without control) we must, as I have just said, constantly re-analyse the rhythmical landmarks of every agility-piece, and must do this again and again.

To make this form of memorizing clear (for it is the rhythmical memory which is here in question), let me give you an example:

The lecturer here demonstrated this point, taking a portion of *Schubert's Impromptu in E flat*. (The passages were played through up to time, but with slight pauses *before* the "rhythmical landmarks".)

You see, you have to guide the piece by landmarks—either once in each bar or three times in each bar—or, as I feel it here, by feeling the time-place of the first and the *third* of each bar as such landmarks:

EXP. 4. SCHUBERT, IMPROMPTU.

Thus I here feel five notes leading up to the third of the bar, and then two notes towards the first of the next bar. To practise the passage, I should pause slightly before the first note of each bar, and again before the seventh note, so as to enable me clearly to recognize, or re-recognize, what coming sound and note it is, and what piano key it is, and what finger it is that precisely *belongs there*. It is even unnecessary to play this next note—the one on the beat. Provided I have *thought* it, I have successfully practised it, and this without actually sounding it at all!

The slow practice fetish.

In the old days "slow practice" was recommended for this purpose. But, obviously, merely sounding the notes slowly in succession will not help in the least. It is the landmarks which have to be learnt! To maintain "mastery" over a piece you must recur again and again to this particular form of practice—this rhythmical re-recognizing of the passage. Slow practice, without this in view, is only a useless fetish.

On learning Fingering.

This grouping of notes in memorizing and in playing rhythmically has its counterpart, when we come to the learning of fingering. As I have said in "Musical Interpretation" (page 122): "The pupil will have no difficulty in *remembering* fingerings, once he grasps the fact that it is not *this* finger or *that* finger which matters, but that it is always a finger-group which is in question—either a complete group or an incomplete one".

In a word, the act of memorizing fingering consists in *associating* a certain set of fingers with a certain set of notes; notes, in the sense of sounds and also in the sense of their connected keyboard positions, or consecutions. "This precisely defines the process, which is therefore an act of *mental association* like every other form of memorizing, thus: Sound—Key—Finger."

In "Pianist's First Music Making", Book II, I have closely shown the process and routine of memorizing and learning the scale fingerings on this principle of grouping.* The reader is here also referred to "The Principles of Fingering and Pedalling" extracted from my "Relaxation Studies" (Bosworth & Co.); also to "Double Third Scales, their Fingering and Practice" (Joseph Williams).

Wrong-note splashing.

Moreover, apart from the mere knowledge of the text, even the successful sounding of the right notes often resolves itself into a question of memory, pure and simple. Here I will read you another short extract from "Musical Interpretation" (page 53):

"It is of no use trying to correct the playing of wrong notes or 'split' notes, merely by telling the pupil to be 'more careful'—this may happen to have some happy result, or it may catastrophically make the pupil more nervous. The only true correction is always to point out the *cause* of the fault. That is, the psycho-physiological cause of the fault. . . ."

Such playing of wrong notes often arises simply from *non-remembrance* of what should be the right succession of notes at the moment, and such memory failure therefore often arises from a totally wrong musical outlook.

Here realize that you should always think the music from the bass upwards, and not from the *treble downwards* and realize, also, that you cannot recall a *mentally-detached* bass note any more than you can recall or remember any other isolated fact or circumstance *if you detach it from its memory-suggestions* or associations. The only true correction of such bass-note *guessing* (and failing) is therefore to insist on realizing the *musical-succession* of the bass-notes themselves—see that they are always noticed and noted as such—that is, as *progressions of the Bass.* Here again, as in fact everywhere, you see how the element of *progression* faces us. Here it is the progression of each Bass-sound from and to its neighbouring Bass-sound which must be noted, and thus musically fixed on the memory-tablets—which indeed is the only way in which any sounds can be memorized musically. Moreover, you must also insist on feeling the actual physical progression of the bass notes on the keyboard. Hence the basses, in playing, must be remembered both as musical and as keyboard successions, and must not be thought of as a wild "grabbing into unknown space", downwards from the melody—in any case a proceeding totally against all laws of Key-treatment!

*"The Pianist's First Music Making" with Duets for Pupil and Teacher, by Felix Swinstead and Tobias Matthay, in three books. (Anglo-French Series.)

(The lecturer here gave as an example a Waltz by Chopin, as he had heard it played at a young ladies' school concert in 1880, with most of the Bass-notes misfired.)

Besides the question of incorrect Bass-note playing, the question of right notes (non-stumbling) also again resolves itself largely into a recognition and memory of the correct progressions on the keyboard. It is of no use trying to recall each note as such; we must on the keyboard *feel* each note as a horizontal progression from each last one—we must recognize its physical "whence-ness" on the keyboard as well as its rhythmical "towards-ness" as to time-place.

(This was again illustrated by the same Waltz in D flat, correctly played.)

Apart from the fact that Memory itself comes under the category of Progression-phenomena, we have seen how the idea of progression helps us to understand the very nature of Phrasing—the very life of music; and how we cannot accurately "place" even the *inside* notes of a Pulse unless we constantly insist upon the keen realization of this element of "towards-ness" or "onwardness"; and further, that it still applies even in the case where figures and phrases have unaccented endings, as I have shown you elsewhere.*

Keeping the "long line" in view.

"Moreover, we found that not only must one think towards sound in the key-descent, and 'towards' pulse, and towards phrase-climax, one must also think towards the greater crisis-points of the larger Shape-outlines, for the same law still applies. That is, we must always have a continuous travelling towards well-noted musical landmarks, and the proportions of these smaller details of movement must nevertheless all the time be strictly subservient to those *larger outlines*, themselves wrought by this constant principle of Progression or Growth."

"Now, success in this respect (this keeping the large outlines clear, and playing in 'long lines') resolves itself again in the end purely into a question of—Memory. Whether we are laying out a large movement or a small one, it is absolutely essential that we should vividly remember, *as we come to it*, the exact proportion of *musical importance* attaching to each of its component sections and climaxes, to its variously contrasting subjects, sentences, phrases, ideas, down to the actual importance of *each note* as part of the complete Whole—only in this way can we keep the long lines of a piece intact.

*From "Musical Interpretation", page 54.

"Only by such perfect *memory* of all its constituents can we hope to produce a musical picture perfect in its perspective, perfect in its outlines—perfect as a *whole*."

Good and bad practice.

This kind of memory is, indeed, the hardest task of the player—and I think it really is harder in our art than in any other. This brings up for consideration what it is that constitutes the difference between good practice and bad practice—the difference between futile automatic practice, and profitable, intelligent practice; in fact, what constitutes correct *presence of mind* in practising the technique of a piece. The musical sense can be perceived without touching the keyboard. But good "technical" practice consists in the effort keenly to locate (or re-locate) the place of each note; that is, its place as to the keyboard, and also its place as to Rhythm. Good technical practice, indeed, consists in trying keenly to recognize *how* each note exists—in its keyboard succession, and where precisely it lives in the consecution of the Time-impulses of the piece; in short, a trying keenly to perceive both the keyboard and Time successions. Good technical practice is a trying to see *where* and *when* each note lives—so that we shall be able alertly and clearly to direct the eventual performance of the piece—because we then really know its material substance. Such practice, therefore, manifestly is a purely mental effort. If all this is not being done, then it is bad practice—in fact, Un-practice.

CODA. We realize, then, that memorizing is purely a matter of "Association"; and however much this very common-sense term, "Association", may be loathed by some of the later psychologists, we are compelled to use it here.

The acquisition of any knowledge, the very act of mastering ideas and making them part of our mind, and the resultant possession of ample and serviceable "apperception-masses"—i.e., masses of serviceable accumulated experiences—all depends on this act of Association, on our thus widening and extending the *Progression-possibilities* of our minds.

We have to make progression-roads from ideas previously in our minds to new ideas, and the new ideas in turn become "progression-possibilities" of our minds. Thus they are memorized—thus they are learnt. In short, the process of memorizing and learning consists of associating ideas, for you cannot learn or memorize without making associations. Such Associations, moreover, cannot be made without Attention and Interest—and this again implies *observation*. Observation in turn implies Analysis, and it is only through Analysis therefore that we perceive anything. Hence also you see the relationship of all these things.

But while admitting the immense value of the habit of *observation*, we must not be blind to its possible pitfalls. Every good thing can be abused and degraded into a mere fetish! Realize that our physical brain-surfaces have really quite definite limits—limits of course differing greatly with different individuals; but with us all, the brain has a limit to its impression-receiving possibilities.

There is some compensation certainly in the fact that as we grow older we, as it were, sum up or condense the various groups of knowledge-ideas in our possession, and when they are thus successfully garnered and stored in our subconsciousness we are able to discard much of the detail—thus again setting free part of our brain-surfaces for further acquisitions. As Alexander Bain has said: "Knowledge in the end signifies knowledge of where in our minds to find it". Nevertheless, after all due economizing of brain-space, the limits of each particular brain are bound to assert themselves.

Hence it behoves us to have a care *how* we fill up these available impression-surfaces of our minds. Indeed, the habit of all-round *observation* is useful, and Mind-widening in its effect—yet we must be careful to *leave room* for the impressions particularly useful in our own individual lives.

Observation-habit, solely for its own sake, may otherwise prove anything but a blessing! We may fill our minds with memories of quite useless things, to the exclusion of things really needed by us—"Pelmanism" may go mad!

To render Observation useful (as it should be), it is needful to make up our minds *what* to observe, what to look for, and what to analyse. It is useless going round a room, observing every corner of it, when we have forgotten what was the object we came to look for in that room. Let us have a clear idea as to the things we wish to be clear upon, and then employ Observation to help us in a useful quest. Observation directed by *knowledge* is the desideratum. Professor Adams has clinched this matter in some aphoristic phrases, page 143 of his "Herbartian Psychology". He says: "Knowledge comes last in order, but it is first in importance. It is knowledge that directs observation (or should direct observation) and gives it *meaning*".

To SUM UP: Realize, that to memorize anything you must make associations, through a process of analysis. Anything to be memorized must mentally be connected-up with something leading to it—you have to accustom you mind-way to a particular sequence of suggestions.

On the other hand, to make use of the mind-ways thus acquired, you must be careful to *allow* these suggestion-sequences to act unimpeded and undisturbed. Therefore, you must never (in a frenzy of fear) permit yourself to try to test "whether you know" something ahead. On the contrary, you must keep your mind on the business in hand, which should be the meticulously adequate sounding of the note or set of notes *due* that moment—and the next will then automatically and surely loom up in your mind.

Here, again, we are faced with that first law of all playing, the necessity for the closest possible *rhythmical* attention to every note, so that each may fall into its precise rhythmical place, and tone-place musically; the precise place where Music mood dictates it must live—whether in straight-time successions or in Rubato-curve successions.

In short, your mind must be concerned with what should be played *that moment*—as part of the Whole; your mind should be concerned with musical sense, vividly alert for the sound and time-place of every required note, through the rhythmical sense and key-sense. Provided this is done, you never risk interfering with the required memory-ways, and you will acquire more and more confidence in the reliability of your own mind; and without which dependability and confidence it is impossible to achieve successful Music-making.

As a last word: First force your mind to recognize the particular sequential actions required, and then allow it, undisturbed, to work in these acquired and therefore safe sequences.

January 1926. TOBIAS MATTHAY.

Additional Note—I.

"On Memory Scratches", from "Teaching Problems".

In *memorizing*, or learning anything, one of the main points to bear in mind is: *avoid making any wrong progressional-impressions* on your mind.

If you make a wrong scratch on your memory-tablets (however slight the scratch) it will take much painful labour, afterwards, to erase the mis-impression; it will take much unnecessary labour therefore before we can *begin* to substitute the right impression for the wrong one.

Such a wrong scratch is almost as bad as slightly exposing a photographic film by accident—it renders the chance of a clear impression on that plate, afterwards, a very precarious matter. This applies everywhere, and all the time. It is so easy to *mis-practise* in this way—sloppily—without noticing, at the time, what damage one is doing to one's Memory-surfaces! Remember, each and every experience is more or less lastingly impressed on the mind; hence it behoves us carefully to present to the mind only the *right successions*. How persistent all impressions are (however difficult it may often seem wilfully to recall them) was brought home to me in a walk recently. I happened to swing my walking-stick rather awkwardly, and suddenly up-flashed a memory of my first walk with my very *first* walking-stick, one which I had myself bought round the corner of our road for fourpence! I must have been about six or seven years of age then! Nevertheless, that awkward swing of my present-day stick served to make me clearly recall and vividly see that first stick, a chocolate painted one, with a cream handle, and with gashes carved on it, filled in with the same reddish-chocolate colour; and I keenly recalled walking down our street at Clapham, and the dullness of the day, and the awkwardness of trying to swing the new stick round, "just like a grown-up", as I imagined at the time. It was a perfectly vivid picture of the stick, and the street, and remembrance of the mood of that moment—more than a half century ago—that flashed up, and I do not remember recalling either the episode or thinking of that stick between-whiles! The impression was still there, although locked away under millions of later impressions. Yet, given the required touch of association and there it was, disclosed, still there, persisting as vividly as if it had happened yesterday! You see, this was no particularly striking episode to persist like that. It merely shows you how *all* impressions remain permanently—though most are smothered over, maybe never to be uncovered!

The Moral is, be careful in practising, *never* to present the wrong physical or musical *succession* to your mind. Always present only the correct succession—the correct Movement mentally, and you can save years of wasted practice time, and worse.

Additional Note—II.

Should the copy be used in public or not?

This question is often asked. The answer is that it must depend on the individual case. Clearly, so long as one has to depend upon the written text it is impossible to give one's mind fully to the sense of the music itself. In fact, one can say, positively that it is quite impossible to give a really adequate performance, musically, unless all the music material has been so fully mastered that it has indeed really been memorized. Again, one's musical freedom may, in a measure, be hampered by the presence of the copy in front of one's eyes during performance, and its presence in some cases is apt to weaken one's self-reliance. My opinion used to be, therefore, that playing "without book" should be imperative; and for those who possess a "natural memory" there is also no question that on most occasions that is best.

However, I have of late years somewhat modified my view on this matter. I have come to the conclusion that for those artists who are inclined to doubt the certainty of their memory it would perhaps be far wiser for such to have the courage to fly in the face of what, after all, is a mere fashion, and to use the copy in public—while, if possible, avoiding the disturbing influence of someone turning the leaves. I feel sure that many a quite fine artist often fails to play his best simply owing to such distrust of his memory! Possibly his memory-powers may really be quite good, but once the demon of "fear-motiv" has been allowed to creep in, collapse can easily be brought about by (as I have shown) the trick of arresting the natural consecution of the memory-impulses and thus "stopping" the memory. Obviously, under such adverse conditions it is impossible to give one's whole mind to the search for the spirit of the music and its translation into sound.

Therefore, in such cases it would seem best to choose the least of two evils, and the presence of the copy on the desk would make for the comfort of the artists themselves and of their audiences; and it would help to give them presence of mind on their work and absence of mind from all untoward considerations.

Madame Clara Schumann, who was a very fine artist, suffered a good deal in this respect, and often used to sit on her copy as a measure of safeguard! Raoul Pugno, a more recent artist, had the courage to act in the common-sense way of placing his copy on the desk, and I recommend it to others similarly conditioned.

November, 1926.